a grandparents'
memory book

" did you really walk five miles to school?"

a grandparents'
memory book

" did you really walk five miles to school?"

compiled by Teri Harrison

*Thanks to all the grandchildren
who generously shared with me their love,
concern and heartfelt
admiration for their grandparents.*

-Teri Harrison

Published by The Grandparent Gift Co. Inc., Alpharetta, GA 30005, www.grandparentgiftco.com

Printed and Bound in the Republic of Korea
Printed by Doosan Printing

Cover photo: Copyright © Chicago Historical Society, 1958,
photographer-Southtown Economist

ISBN 1-882835-37-9

Designed By: Cooper Smith & Co.

—————— • ——————

Dedication

To all the grandparents who will
give their grandchildren the richest gift
of all — their memories.

A Grandchild's Wish

Have I ever told you about the gift
I'd love from you?

It's a gift you'll never find
in any mall or store.
But nonetheless a gift,
I'll treasure and adore.

It's a gift that fits all sizes,
one I don't already own.
And it's something only you can give,
only you and you alone.

It's a gift you carry with you,
every hour of the day.
You can take it out and share it,
then tuck it back away.

It's a gift I vow to share,
with children of my own.
And proudly make a treasure,
in my heart and in my home.

It's a gift I'll always keep,
as long as I shall live.
For your memories are the richest gift,
you could ever give.

-Teri Harrison

Table of Contents

———— • ————

$\mathscr{I}$ntroduction

Memories are like fingerprints — unique impressions of who we are as individuals. Of all the wonderful gifts grandparents shower upon grandchildren, nothing compares with the gift of memories. Memories are a gift of heart and soul that only you can give.

One of life's greatest wonders is the relationship between grandparents and grandchildren. The two generations share an unconditional love and joy in the treasures unique to their generation. *A Grandparents' Memory Book—Did You Really Walk Five Miles to School?* shares the best of both generations. When this gift is read by a grandparent, they are delighted with the fresh, honest, curious questions posed by grandchildren of all ages. Here are questions real grandchildren want answered about their grandparents' lives — some funny, some touching, some insightful, just like grandchildren themselves. When a grandparent completes the book and gives it to their grandchildren, a gift of a lifetime is being exchanged — a gift of family, roots, memories of the past, and wishes for the future.

Why are your grandparents'
memories important to you?

Grandparents have firsthand
knowledge of a time that we can only
learn about in history books.
If we are lucky enough to know our
grandparents we should spend time
with them — they have so much
to give us.

Cathie Rutkin, 31

family history

Where did our family come from? (Explain.)

Thomas Allen, 18

*M*y grandparents symbolize the roots and places that I come from.

Jonathan Vass, 16

Did you spend the night at your Grandma and Grandpa's house?

Shannon Lee, 3 1/2

What is your fondest memory of Grandpa/Grandma?

Kristyn Berghoefer, 21

What physical characteristics, personality traits or skills have you seen run through generations of our family?

Lynn Maas, 46

What did your grandparents do?
(for a living)

Marc Goodman, 16

What is the best lesson you learned from your parents? What values that your parents taught you did you pass (or try to) on to your children?

Stacey Wagoner, 21

I would like to know more about my grandparents' lives because they are my ancestors, they are a part of me.

Robert Moroto, 8

When were you born? Where were you born?

Daniel Welch, 9

Were you named after anyone in particular?
What is the story behind how you were named?

Ty Lee, 34

> *F*amilies are the most important relationship we'll have in life. Grandparents have a lifetime of experience to share. Mine have taught me and entertained me with their stories.
>
> *Angela L. Morrison, 25*

Did you get along with your siblings? (Explain.)

Angie Nyce, 27

Did you have family activities you did together? (Explain.)

Angie Nyce, 27

It's important to know how kids spent their time many years ago. What my grandparents remember is important because it was a special part of their life. When I am old, I would like someone to be interested in what I do now when I'm a child.

Trevor Woolever, 11

childhood years

Where did you live when you were little?

Alexandra McNay, 7

Did you have a big backyard when you were little?

Michael Daus, 6

Did you have crayons?

Gage Gesiriech, 7

Did you have your own room when you were little?

Jocelyn Reist, 5

_____

_____

_____

_____

_____

_____

_____

_____

Did you ever jump on your bed when you were little?

Michael Epstein, 6

_____

_____

_____

_____

It seems neat to know how you lived so far back in time. It sounds like fun!

Allison Stevens, 8

What was your favorite meal?
Who fixed that meal?

Sarah Joy Staude, 19

Did you eat carrots when you were
7 years old?

Kelsey Case, 6

Did you have popsicles when you
were little?

Taylor Snell, 5

*B*ecause
I love them
and they were
born before
me, I want to
know how
their lives were
different when
they were kids.

Taylor Waldorf, 7

Did you ever go out to dinner or did you
eat at home?

Elizabeth Leruth, 11

What did you look like when you
were little?

Alexandra McNay, 7

Did you ever play card games? (Which ones?)

Michael Epstein, 6

What was your favorite game?

Allison Stevens, 8

*A*ll the stories that they tell are just so awesome to hear and they are so interesting. I could listen to their stories forever.

Caleb Nelson, 17

What did you do for fun? Did you run, did you jump and play?

Jessie Krause, 8

Did you play any sports? (Tell me about them.)

Brett Middlekauff, 9

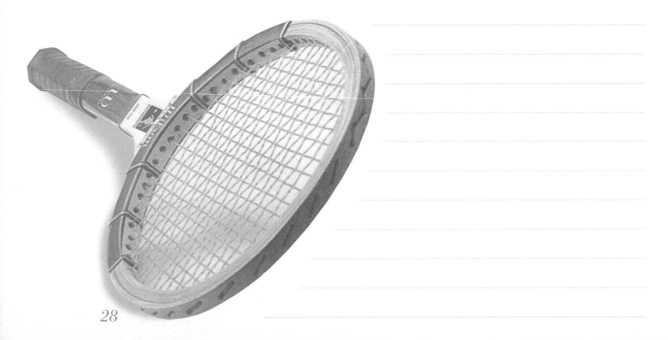

What kind of kid were you? Did you stay inside or play and build forts and things?

Josh Heissman, 18

How did you make friends?

Katelyn Reef, 7

I'd like to know more about their lives because it makes a connection between generations. Making me realize they were just like me in many ways, not a whole new person.

Bre Handley, 15

Did you ever do anything really bad when you were a kid? If so, what was it?

Sarah Field, 11

What pranks do you remember from childhood?

Beth Tubbs, 35

Did you ever get in trouble for lying?
(Tell me about it.)
Robert Slingsby, 5

Did you and my parents ever fight as
bad as me and my parents?
Luke Henderson, 16

Were you happy as a kid?
Jessica Woodward, 11¹/₂

I am very
close to my
grandparents
and I love
hearing about
their stories.
I love to hear
how they lived
and what
was important
when they
were young.

Michelle Morgan, 22

31

What was the greatest hardship you endured as a child?
Bob Corwin, 34

Who was your childhood hero? Why?
Beverly Pell, 27

What is your favorite childhood memory?

Amy Rhodes, 21

What kind of pets did you have when you were younger?

Brian Walen, 11

What did you always want to be when you "grow up"? What did you turn out to be?

Mallory Primm, 10

What is your favorite holiday? Why?

Teri Harrison, 33

I think it is fun and interesting to learn about my grandparents' lives. You can also learn things from them. I think it is neat to compare things today with things long ago. I like to hear stories from elderly people because they had things so different back when they were a kid.

Sarah Field, 11

What did you do at your house for Thanksgiving? What are some of the favorite foods at Thanksgiving? Maybe cranberries, bread, turkey, mashed potatoes or gravy?

Eric Bowron, 7

What was it like to trick-or-treat at Halloween? What was your favorite costume?

Teri Harrison, 33

Do you remember a special birthday or Christmas? What was the best present you received as a child?

Beth Tubbs, 35

Did you get lots of Christmas presents?

Cassie Helda, 5

When did you open your Christmas presents? Did Santa come to visit you?

Shannon Lee, 3½

*G*randparents are
great teachers for us -
not only about the
ABC's and 123's, but
about our own lives and
selves and families.
Amy E. Schiffer,26

school
years

I like to know what my grandparents lives were like because it's interesting for me to compare their lives as a kid with mine. I like knowing how my grand-parents lived and what their life was like.

Jessica Woodward, 11½

What was a typical school day like as a child? What time did you get up? Any chores?

Joe DeGabriele, 20

Did girls just wear dresses?

Jessica Woodward, 11½

What did you do in your spare time as a teenager?

Adam Fox, 15

Did you really walk five miles to school?
Lacie Edwards, 9

Where did you go to school?
Danielle Ligenza, 9

When you went to school was it kids of all ages in the same classrooms or different classrooms? (Explain.)
Ali Vogel, 10

What was your favorite subject?
Desiree Handley, 16

What type of grades in school did you get?
David Brownson, 18

Was education important to you?
(Why or why not?)
Dana Ritchie, 27

What was your favorite game at recess?
Michelle Wright, 10

What is your best memory of a favorite teacher?
Kris Hartle, 24

Who was your best friend in high school?
Bre Handley, 15

In what activities did you participate in high school?
Allison Wagoner, 17

What is your worst and best memory of high school?

Bre Handley, 15

Did you play any musical instrument? (Which ones?)

Jeffrey Silverberg, 12

What was your favorite movie as a teenager?

Johana Martin, 17

How much was it to go to the movies?

Bailey Gesiriech, 9

Their memories are so important to me because I know when I ask them to look back to their past, a smile will lighten their face. Nothing pleases me more than to see my grandparents smile.

David Brownson, 18

49

What kind of dances did you do as a teenager?
Tiffany Snyder, 25

Did you go to the prom? (Tell me about it.)
Fatima Razavi, 15

Where was your favorite hangout as a kid?
David Brownson, 18

What clothes did you wear?

Allison Bryant, 6

How did you entertain yourself without many (or any) electronic toys?

Stephanie Anderson, 11

Did your parents give you curfews and what time was it?

William Bleu George, 10 and Barbi George, 38

It is interesting to know what life was like at the time when my grandparents were my age, and it is fun to compare those times with today.

Cindy Pape, 19

51

How old were you when you were allowed
to have your first girlfriend/boyfriend?
Lindsay Ansari, 12

What were dates like?
Cindy Pape, 19

*I*think
their lives
were different
than my life.

Katelyn Reef, 7

When did you first fall in love?
Elizabeth Leruth, 11

What was your first car?
Reid Sneddon, 10

How much was a car in those days?

Brad Donnelly, 10

Did you have an after school job? (Describe it.)

Omar Shah, 14

I want to know more about my grandparents' lives because I find it interesting how people had to live a long time ago. Also my grandparents have many cool stories.

Jon Putnins, 12

work, love & family

My grandparents are important to me because they were the reason I was born. They had my parents, and my parents had me. Their memories are important to me because they are part of my family and I love to hear stories about them.

Erin Gallo, 10

What was your first job?
Kim Kurtz, 36

How much did you get paid for your first job?
Jordan Sukut, 11

What is the "toughest" job you have ever had?
Dan Sennett, 21

What was your favorite job that you had?
Jordan Sukut, 11

When did you leave home? To go where?
Melissa Jensen, 30

How expensive was a college
education when you were young?
Tiffany Snyder, 25

How did you and Grandma/Grandpa meet each other?

Andy Springer, 18

_____

_____

_____

_____

_____

What was your wedding like?

Beth Tubbs, 35

_____

_____

_____

_____

_____

_____

How old were you when you were married?
Dave Kanne, 31

Where did you go on your honeymoon?
Joe DeGabriele, 20

When did you buy your first house?
Dave Kanne, 31

How much was a home?

Joel Krempasky, 10

Did any wars affect your life? If so, how?

Annie Skaron, 10

If you were ever in a war, how old were you then?

Jamey Bryant, 8

How did the Great Depression affect the way you spent or saved your money?

Michelle Wright, 10

How old were you when you had your first child? Your last?

Christy Panepinto, 14 and Brianna Panepinto, 9

Were you nervous about being parents? (Explain.)

Sarah Johnson, 21

Was it hard to raise your children? (Why or why not?)

Ashly Ogden, 9

What was my Mom/Dad like?

Kristyn Berghoefer, 21

What kind of trouble did my parents get into as teenagers?

David Brownson, 18

Was it hard when Mom/Dad started driving? (In what way?)

Lindsay Ansari, 12

I would like to know because I could never believe that my mom was a baby.

Sara Wurster, 9

Did you find yourself saying things as a parent, that your parents said, that you swore you would never say? What were they?

Ty Lee, 35

What was your reaction when you found out my Mom and Dad were getting married?

Rachel Cruz, 15

I always ask my Grandma, 'Didn't Mom do that when she was my age?', whenever I do something wrong.

Kristi Nakano, 16

When were you proudest of your children?

Beverly Pell, 27

Grandparents' memories are important because they can teach you about the past.

Crystal Azbell, 7

changing times

Have you ever been on a train?

Tara Hickman, 7

When was your first airplane trip?

Amy Svendsen, 21

Did you have spaceships?

Tyler Yonker, 6

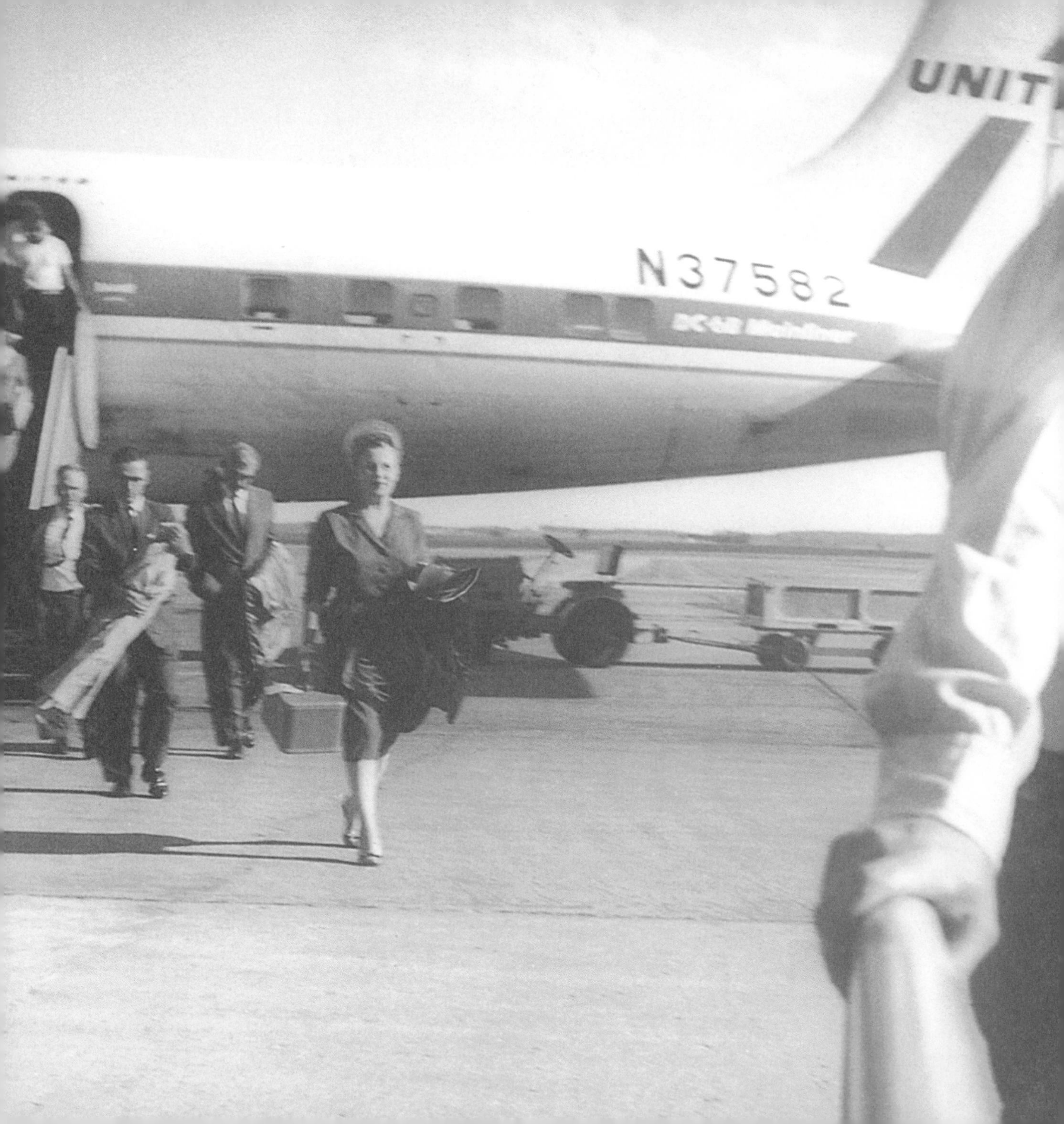
UNIT
N37582

What did you do when the first man landed on the moon?
Eric Gerber, 10

Who was President when you were born?
Eric Gerber, 10

How much was a cheeseburger when you were younger?
Josh Heissman, 18

Do you remember when stores were closed on Sundays? What year did they open for business on Sundays?

Christy Panepinto, 14 and Brianna Panepinto, 9

When did they say smoking is bad?

Dakota Fisher, 8

How much was a bottle of Coke when you were a kid?

Taylor Holt, 11

I would like to know more about my grandparents' lives because it is fun to know what was happening in the world before I was born.

Brian Walen, 11

If you could keep one thing from your childhood the same, what would it be?

Kristyn Berghoefer, 21

Was life as fast as it is now?

David Freedman, 15

Grandparents have a very personal link to the past. It is fun to learn history when it's about someone you know and love.

Kristi Green, 17

How old were you when television was invented?
Tyler Cole, 9

How much did your first TV cost?
Nate Hartle, 24

What did you do without air conditioning?
Tara Hickman, 7

What invention or scientific achievement has impressed you most in the 20th century? Why?

Connie Ventress, 39

How do you feel about computers?

Michelle McInerney, 21

I've always been interested in history - the time that they were growing up is one I'm very curious about.

Lisa McGregor, 36

79

I would like
to know more about
my grandparents so
I could remember
them by heart.
They are my friends.
Christopher Snyder, 7

life
questions

Who was your role model? Who influenced your life in the most significant way?

Tiffany Snyder, 25

Rick & Jack

When did you decide what you wanted to be in life?

Amber Benjamin, 17

What was your biggest dream in life? Did it come true?

Desiree Handley, 16

_____

_____

_____

_____

_____

_____

What were your life's disappointments? Do you have any regrets? What would you do over?

Julie Mammano, 34

_____

_____

_____

_____

_____

_____

I believe we learn about ourselves every time we hear about our grandparents' lives, adventures, dreams, etc. Without them -- we wouldn't be. They deserve our utmost respect.

Beverly Pell, 27

Do you miss anything that is no longer available now? (What and why?)

Melinda Mergen, 22

What hobbies do you enjoy?

Peter Braunz, 14

What is your favorite place to visit?

Anne Bloom, 22

What is your favorite book?

Tyler Schultz, 5

What civic clubs/groups have you belonged to? Why?

Sarah Joy Staude, 19

Where are all the places you have lived or traveled to?

Sarah Johnson, 21

_____

_____

_____

_____

_____

_____

_____

What have you always wanted to do that you never got to do?

Johana Martin, 17

_____

_____

_____

_____

What were the best times of your life?

Melinda Mergen, 22

I would like to know more about my grandparents' lives so I could know what they had to go through and to know what it was like for them.

Annie Skaron, 10

What values were most important to you?
Teresa L. Miller, 30

What is your most cherished possession and why?
Shanley Rhodes, 27

What was the most difficult transition in your life?

Allison Wagoner, 17

_____

_____

_____

_____

_____

_____

_____

_____

_____

What is the most embarrassing thing you ever did?

Allison Wagoner, 17

_____

_____

_____

_____

What I love most about my grandparents is their ability to understand. I think they received this trait because they have lived for a long time and many radical events have happened during their lifetime.

Fatima Razavi, 15

Grandparents are special.
Each child is given a certain amount.
One can't get more at the store.
Their memories are unique.
Once they're gone you'll never get
another chance to ask any questions.

Kristen Przeklasa, 15

What I love most about my
grandparents is that I can go to their
house whenever I want, because
I'm not just a visitor, I belong there.

Gina Gabrielli, 16

life as a grandparent

How did you feel when you first found out you were going to be a grandparent?
Jess Rodriguez, 16

_____

_____

_____

_____

_____

_____

How did you guys get to know me?
Eric Bowman, 7

_____

_____

_____

_____

_____

_____

_____

I love the fact that no matter what happens to me, I know that my grand-parents will always love me.

Katie Brittle, 14 1/2

94

Did you want your child to raise your grandkid the same way you raised them? Why/why not?

Jess Rodriguez, 16

Do you look anything like me?

Gina Gabrielli, 16

Is there anything about me that reminds
you of yourself?
Angela L. Morrison, 25

Do you see anything in me that reminds
you of my parents? (Explain.)
Jane Thomas, 50

How much do you love me?
Hannah Rasmussen, 6

Do you see a change in children today compared to when your own children were young? If so, what and why?

Kari Kanne, 29

What did you learn from your grandparents that you incorporate into your grandparenting style today?

Katie Ericson, 21

What's your favorite thing about being a grandparent?

Johana Martin, 17

What have you learned most about life from being a grandparent?

Jess Rodriguez, 16

*M*y grandma and grandpa give me the most love.

Bijan Bonakdar, 6

My grandpa
makes me laugh
and play

Bryan Phillips, 5

My grandma
spoils me.

Allyson Smart, 5

special
questions
for
grandma
and grandpa

What did Grandpa do to win you over?

Sabrina Nouacer, 15

_____

_____

_____

_____

_____

_____

_____

_____

Did you want to go to work or stay home and take care of children?

Jessica Lawler, 30

_____

_____

_____

_____

_____

What has been your biggest thrill as a grandfather?
Todd Goehring, 29

Did you ever play with your dolls?
Bijan Bonakdar, 6

Did you go fishing?
Braden Lee, 8

Did you have a collection when you were a little boy?
Darcie Fisher, 6

Did you ever play baseball?
Jon Putnins, 12

I would like to know about my grandparents' lives because they have been in the world for a very long time. They have a great deal of wisdom about things and they can give good advice.

Sarah Johnson, 21

the older generation

How old were you when your hair started turning color?

Nate Gilbertson, 7

Were you afraid to be old?

Kristi Nakano, 16

Do you still feel young?

Gina Gabrielli, 16

When did you feel you were starting to get older? Do you like being older than younger?

Taylor Waldorf, 7

How does it feel to watch your children become old and have children on their own?

John Hopkins, 18

What do you think happens when we die?

Desiree Handley, 16

*G*randmas are old and sometimes have to have a little cane.

Lindsay Chambers, 4

*M*any times, memories
are all we have to remember
someone…someone who
won't be around forever.
We have such a limited time
with them, you have to get
all you can while you can.

Monika Hohn, 22

the
future

Do you have any special skills or traits that you could teach me or that I could learn?

Jonathan Vass, 16

What is your advice for me as I am getting ready for college?

David Brownson, 18

What I love about my grandparents is that they seem to be the smarter of generations and most wise. I always ask them for advice and they are very interesting people.

Kristi Nakano, 16

If you could give me one gift (not literal gift), what would it be?

Amy Rhodes, 21

In your opinion, what really matters in life?

Sandra Mittry, 40

What do you want your great-grandchildren to know about you?

Angela L. Morrison, 25

What do you want to get out of the rest of your life?

Michelle Morgan, 22

What hopes do you have for your children and grandchildren?

Michelle Morgan, 22

Grandparents have a lot of experience - the experience may have been long ago, but it's still relevant. Grandparents help us to see that time does heal wounds. They have a longer perspective on life.

Linda Shepard, 34

115

my questions for you

(Blank pages for grandchildren
to add their own questions for
their grandparents to answer.)